Get Married In 12 Months

This Book is a
Gift

To

From

On the occasion of

Date

You are Special

JOE IGBOANUGO

GET

MARRIED

IN 12 MONTHS

31 common assumption exposed
31 answers to crirital questions provided
24 powerful pointers to your potential spouse

Get Married In 12 Months

A Marriage Revolution Book

Copyright © 2012

Joe Igboanugo

ISBN 978-978-50768-0-6

Published by

Transformation. MEDIA

Port Harcourt, Nigeria.

Tel: +234(0)8097 739 229

E-mail: transformbybooks316@yahoo.com

Unless otherwise indicated, all scripture quotations are from the New King James Version of the Holy Bible.

Printed in the Federal Republic of Nigeria, 2016

Gospel Warehouse Tel+234 802 325 5362

Nigeria. good people, good nation

Graphics:

VIVIDSTAR ⭐

+234 803 421 4854, +234 802 309 7299

Dedication

To all singles who are passionate about getting married and willing to go God's way;

To all parents who desire to see their children get married and live fulfilled;

To all pastors, marriage counselors and intercessors who labor to see quality families emerge

Acknowledgments

First and foremost I thank my Abba Father, the sole initiator of marriage and family system for the inspirations contained in this book.

My wife and best friend for life Meg (Sweet) for "making things easier" when I proposed marriage to her some fourteen years ago; getting married to you has made our ministry to marriages an exciting one. Thanks for encouraging me to "push out" this book.

All my associates and lovely brethren at Gospelland (Changers International Church); and MarriageRevolution Outreach, I appreciate you all.

I cannot appreciate you enough, Ray Uzuegbu my coordinator in Accra, Ghana for your large heartedness. You converted stress to fun throughout the period of my interactive research on relationships in Ghana.

What can I say about Rev. George Izunwa, the empowerment pastor, your support over the years has been immense.

My father in the Lord, Bishop Yomi Isijola and Mama Rev Mrs. Esther Isijola, your wisdom and impartation have provided us a strong shoulder with which to climb higher.

I will not fail to acknowledge the enormous pioneering contributions of Dr Don Odunze Snr and Pastor Bimbo Odukoya, (both of blessed memories) in the area of relationships and marriages. Your works are still speaking today.

Dr Stephanie Oarhe, Pastor Chris Ojigbani, Dr Don Odunze Jnr. and many others, thank you for your labors as God keeps using you to direct our youths.

My mentor extra-ordinary, Dr Steve Ogan and his amiable wife Atim I thank you for setting the pace in balanced biblical counseling on marriage relationships.

Content

Find

**a good spouse
you find good life
and even more: the
favor of God.**

-Proverbs 18:22 (MSG)

www.marriagerevolution316.org

Introduction

It has been said that you make your choices, and then your choices make you. The choice of life partner has become the most important decision any believer is faced with after the choice of Jesus Christ as Lord and personal Savior. Your choice in marriage leaves you with life- term consequences that will either let you fulfill destiny or truncate it. People who either took this for granted or didn't know how to go about it today live in different shades of regrets. Divorce regrettably is now on the increase even in the body of Christ than ever before. It has become evident that more adults now die of marital-stress induced ailmentsthan other sicknesses. It ought not to be so.

An anonymous author once asserted, "Marriage can either be a wind that lifts your wings or an albatross that hangs your neck down". Some couples who live in difficult marriage relationships today have traced their pains and agony to either ignorance or negligence of basics as regards finding a life partner.

Apart from wisdom to choose rightly; many lovely, hardworking and God-fearing mature singles have not been able to connect to their life partners. Why? Others find it difficult to keep and nurture a relationship unto marriage.

Much learning, electronic media, movies, civilization and many other factors have made it more challenging for our youths to trace godly values and the Word of God concerning relationships. It is amazing the kind of factors people submit to when choosing life partners. From physiological to psychological; from traditional to spiritual; from circumstantial to irrational as much as from economic to social. I have grouped my findings into two categories, major and minor. Some as much as they sound self- indulgent, outlandish and obsolete seem to have "worked" for some people. For others it had either delayed or frustrated their lofty dream of a good married life.

Major:

Physical Appearance

Voice/smile

Talent/gift Career

Type Spiritual

Conviction

Personality/carriage

Character

Others ~ she/he is my childhood friend, etc

Minor:

Tribe/nationality

Family Name

Parental Influence

Respected Opinions

Religious/denominational

Wealth

Accidental ~ pregnancy

Others ~ in order to obtain resident permit/green card, etc.

Ignorance has destroyed more relationships than any other factors. Lack of adequate information and good understanding has delayed more singles than lack of praying and fasting.

The purpose of Get Married In 12 Months is to provide practical biblical counsel, necessary social common sense and basic spiritual power (anointing) needed by any single man or woman to get married.

Secondly, to assist singles make the right choice and avoid obvious pitfalls in marriage.

Thirdly, in my own little way, to make available some relevant information to relationship therapists and pastors involved in marriage issues.

Read and Get Married SUCCESSFULLY!!

Chapter One

MINDSET FOR MARRIAGE

A good man brings good things out of the good stored up in him, and the evil man brings evil things out of the evil stored up in him.

The principles of physical maturity, emotional maturity, financial stability and spiritual maturity still stand as powerful pointers to readiness for marriage. Moving further with the combination of these and more brings us to an essential aspect of man that determines the kind of result he produces.

Your general attitude, and the way you think about things and make decisions define your mindset (courtesy, Longman Dictionary of Contemporary English, (c) Pearson 2008). Your mindset will affect your choice of life partner and how well you relate and enjoy your spouse. Very sorry to say, some people's belief system about marriage and life.

partner is not only archaic but in disagreement with the Word of God. While some maintain a ridiculous view which they term modern or civilized approach; others draw inspirations from their culture and traditions.

You must renew your mind2 with the word of God and be willing to boldly work towards a happy home with all sincerity and purpose. Our mindset is formed by inert belief system generated by the information we receive over time plus our environment of influence.

> Don't copy the behavior and customs of this world
> but let God transform you into a new person by
> changing the way you think. The Holy Bible.

The Way Forward

Catch the vision of an ideal home. An ideal home is a godly, happy, and lovely marriage relationship (not necessarily a beautiful house) between one man and one woman in the first instance, and then with happy, healthy and godly children; altogether, fulfilling God's peculiar mandate for their home. Every home is unique and has a unique assignment from God.

Your family background may not be the best example of an ideal home but your vision can change it!

Are you from a polygamous home? Are you a product of a broken home or brought up by a single parent? Are your parents still living together? How friendly?

I know a couple for a period of about ten years when the children were growing up between the ages of 9-23, never rode in one car together to any occasion. The man always blamed the woman for any wrongdoing, by the children even in their presence. He never sat down with the family for relaxation. He never visited the children at school even though he provided for them. Can you imagine the environment under which these children grew up?

Another case is where the wife left the husband with the children and relocated to another city in pursuit of business and contracts. These kids grew up seeing their mum once in a blue moon.

What model of homes do you think will exist in the mind's picture of these children?

12 Questions You Should Not Ignore

1. **What kind of models are your parents?**

You must not repeat the mistakes of your parents for whatever reason. If they have a good relationship, you must improve on it! You had no choice where you were born into, but you have a choice whom to spend the rest of your life with and whether to enjoy or merely endure it.

2.   What Can The Society Give To You?

What we watch today on cathode ray tubes (TV/Internet) are not real reflections of marriage relationship and family values. There is a lot of cosmetics and perversion in Hollywood, Nollywood, Bollywood etc. even most movie script writers and talk- show presenters are stack unbelievers who have no regards for the sanctity of marriage.

3.   What Are You Looking For In A Life Partner?

Remember that vistas are not virtues. I am a strong advocate of threshold attraction (the fundamental characteristics that attracted you to your partner - whether physical attributes, talents or attitudes) because it helps to maintain stability in a relationship. (See my book, Marriage Revolution). However, you must take to heart that most visible attributes naturally tend to fade with time, (age), use and environment. Move beyond outward beauty or possessions and look for inner virtues.

4. Are You Ready To Share Your Liberty With Another Person?

Most challenges in marriage relationships today are traceable to partners who still want to live their lives as if they owe no one any explanation. As soon as you say 'I do', your time, your money, your body and generally your decisions and choices are shared with your spouse for life. Even your relationships with your family members, friends and in some instances colleagues are shared! The truth is that you don't have secrets anymore.

5. Are You Thinking That She/he Will Change?

A big surprise! People do not usually change much after wedding. In fact the only slight change might be for "worse"! For example if you are courting a quarrelsome person and you keep 'managing', thinking that he/she will change when you eventually marry, you goof! However, good attitudes can be developed with time, patience, knowledge, tolerance and humility. But sincerely speaking what you are thinking about your partner may not be exactly what you will get. Prepare to make the best out of the worst of him/her.

6. Does Marriage Make One Responsible?

Marriage does not make one responsible or achieve self-respect. A responsible person is the one who faces up his challenges without blaming another or building up excuses. In fact marriage exposes one's level of responsibility or integrity. Are you ready for that challenge?

7. Do You Believe Marriage Guarantees You Happiness?

Marriage does not guarantee happiness. It is you that bring happiness and peace into your own home. If you don't learn to be happy as a single person, you will not be happy as a married person.

8. Are You Planning To Copy The Style of You Parents or Other Couples?

Every marriage relationship is unique in itself. It is a combination of the personalities of the spouses plus the Word of God they choose to obey that give identity to any particular marriage/home.

9. What Is Your Idea About Sex?

Some people actually think that marriage is a final solution to sexual desires and immorality. "When I get married, I know I will settle down". If you do not decide to settle down now with some quality parameters guiding your libido, you will be shocked that marriage will expose your weakness or indiscipline. Renewing your mind ahead of time with what the Word says about chastity and self-control is your only guarantee.

10. Does Your Mind Assure You that You Have All It Takes To Get A Life-Partner?

Awareness of one's ability, potential or endowments is not evil, however when your confidence and faith are built on them, it becomes pride. Subtle pride may not be easily noticeable but it breeds presumptions attitude you can't really evaluate people and situations accurately. Meekness is the key irrespective of what you are endowed with, position or possessions. Relate and treat people with respect. Don't be cocky or snobby it repels good things and kills opportunities.

> **Meekness is the key irrespective of your achievements; pride repels good things and kills opportunities**

11. Do you have Inferiority Complex or Low Self- Esteem?

Folks who grew up in an oppressive, intimidated and unfriendly environment tend to be aggressive in their attitude towards others. They are always protective and secretive. Very poor in managing relationships, always thinking the next person looks better, so " let me do something to shore-up". Low self esteem makes one want to compare himself with another- as a result either look down on himself and overestimate the next person or look down on another and rate himself more highly than he is. With this attitude it will be difficult to connect or keep a peaceful marriage relationship.

12. Are You Ready To See Marriage As God Made It?

Marriage is designed for life.

So then, they are no longer two but one flesh. Therefore, what God has joined together, let no man separate. And I say to you, whoever divorces his wife, except for sexual immorality, and marries another, commits adultery; and whoever marries her who is divorced commits adultery.4 Marriage is designed to exist between two persons only.

Therefore a man shall leave his father and mother and be joined to his wife, and they shall become one flesh.

Marriage permits no perversion.

Marriage is honorable among all and the bed undefiled; but fornicators and adulterers God will judge.

Marriage is designed for sexual pleasure.

Sexual drives are strong, but marriage is strong enough to contain them and provide for a balanced and fulfilling sexual life in a world of sexual disorder.

Marriage is designed to multiply a godly legacy on earth.

So God created man in His own image... Male and female He created them. Then God blessed them, and God said to them, "Be fruitful and multiply; fill the earth and subdue it; have dominion

Marriage is designed for companionship.

And the LORD God said, "It is not good that man should be alone; I will make him a helper comparable to him.

Chapter Two

31 COMMON ASSUMPTIONS THAT LEAD TO MISTAKES IN THE CHOICE OF LIFE PARTNERS

Quick! Catch all the little foxes before they ruin the vineyard of your love, for the grapevines are all in blossom.

1. I must marry someone from my town, tribe or church.

    ⊗ There is nothing wrong with marrying within your locality or church denomination. However, God's perfect choice for you may be well outside that box you created. Sincerely let God have His way, provided she/he is born again and fits into your future where she/he hails from counts little.

2. He loves me and I love him that's what matters; I don't care about what people say.

   ✍ Sometimes because you are "in love", you could be dead wrong. Love is not enough. Antecedents, character and focus should be examined. God can also use people to guide you.

3. We quarrel a lot but when we wed I believe it will stop.

   ✍ When you wed your quarrel will graduate to fights!

   Handle your emotions now or BREAK UP!

4. If I don't marry him he said he will die.

   ✍ It is an ancient lie, he will NOT die!

> **Assumptions are the termites
> of relationships.**
> **-Henry Winkler.**

5. He is younger than I am or she is older,
   therefore we can't get married.

   🖎 Age is important but age difference is NOT
   VERY IMPORTANT in a good marriage
   relationship. Just make sure you consider,
   discuss and handle the all- important issues
   of submission and self-respect before you
   proceed.

6. It is not everything about me that I will open
   up to my fiancé. When we get married things
   will sort themselves out.

   🖎 Some who tried this technique in the past
   before they got married now live in pain of
   "betrayal", distrust and disharmony after
   their spouses discovered certain skeletons in

the cupboard. Your past, present and future belong to both of you. Let your partner know all he needs to know, it's his to decide what to do with it. Do not fear to be transparent in everything.

7. I am short, my partner must be tall.

   ✎ Good thinking! But sometimes waiting for a tall partner may make you lose God-sent opportunities.

8. I want to try her if she is good I will marry her.

   ✎ Also give her opportunity to try you out. Trying should not include sex.

9. Her legs are not straight.

   ✎ Charm can mislead and beauty soon fades. The woman to be admired and praised is the one who lives in the fear-of-God.

> Some people think that they can be
> happy only with the person who is the
> best looking, most intelligent, and most
> charming.

10. He is a power-dresser and speaks well. I will marry him.

   ✍ Good dress-sense is beautiful, eloquence is wonderful but none of them has anything to do with quality relationship. Be careful, my dear.

11. He buys me anything I ask, so he loves me.

   ✍ It is also possible that a man could buy whatever a lady asks for because of selfish and ulterior motives. Look out for more immaterial clues with which to determine love.

12. He doesn't have a well-paying job, how can he take care of a wife?

✎ If he doesn't have a well paying job now he can have tomorrow. Is he hard-working, developing himself and shows definitive prospects?

13. Even if the love is not there I will marry him/her for his/her money. After all, what is love without money?

✎ If money is your only determinant factor for love then you are in trouble. Never marry anyone because of material gains.

> **"Trying to get married through a shortcut is like climbing a very tall tree with a worn-out cord."**.

14. Men are heart-breakers. It is very hard to find a husband these days.

✎ What a tragedy to generalize one or few persons' past bad experiences? There are still very good men in search of good wives today. Believe it and see it.

15. Girls from that tribe are materialistic; men from that tribe are not caring.

✍ Never use one person's ugly encounter to decide the pattern of life of a whole region. Materialism does not belong to any particular set of people. Modesty and tender loving care can also be found from anywhere God is revered.

16. Girls who put on trousers and make-up are flirts, therefore cannot make good wives.

✍ Outward appearance has long deceived quite a lot of people. In as much as decency in costume is a virtue, you can't determine quality girls from dress code alone.

17. My fiancée can't prepare a nice dish but with house helps and cooks we can cope when we get married.

≥ If you are someone who loves good food and that is very important to you, then leaving your stomach in the hands of house maids is dangerous. Your fiancée MUST IMPROVE or she might lose you to your cooks in the future.

18. Is his mother still alive? Mother in-laws are witches.

≥ If you believe that all mother in-laws are witches you might never get a "non-witch" spouse. If you wish your mother in-law dead how do you hope to have your own son/daughter in-law?

19. She sings very well. He is a prayer warrior, etc.

≥ Talents or gifts could be deceptive and definitely not the best parameter for determining a good life-partner.

20. He/she is my childhood friend, I can't disappoint him/her now or we have lived

together for four years, I can't leave him/her now.

- ⊗ Neither your childhood nor the four years is anything when compared with your future. If it is NECESSARY, walk away and START right.

21. I am not getting younger anymore, let me just marry him.

- ⊗ It is more blessed to marry the right person at 39 than the wrong person at 21. A bad marriage is much worse than living alone.

22. I am still young I will settle down later.

- ⊗ It is dangerous to toy with opportunities.

23. I will lure him to get me pregnant. That will make him speed up the marriage plans.

- ⊗ That is fornication; that is deception. If he ends up hooked to you, your marriage will exist only by series of deceptions.

24. He still smokes and drinks occasionally but I will convert him when we get married.

   ✎ Habits die hard, says the old maxim. Never marry someone with the mind of changing him/her in the future.

You do not change a person...
no matter how much you love them

---

25. We disagree and quarrel about almost everything but we cannot break-up now. We have gone far with wedding plans.

   ✎ A broken engagement is far better than a broken marriage. Wedding is a one-day event, marriage, a life- long process.

26. If I move in with him, it will hasten our marriage plans.

✎ As a child of God moving in with him in order to hasten wedding arrangements is not an option. Co-habitation is not Christian marriage. The selfish guy says, "why should I marry her when I am getting all the benefits of marriage without the responsibilities.

27. He lives abroad. He promised to marry me when he returns.

✎ Your relationship needs physical closeness to develop and mature. Many ladies have lost out, got older and missed precious opportunities because they were waiting for a guy who promised to marry them and travelled abroad. Phone calls, video/internet call, e-mail are not enough. Act wisely.

28. Spending money on my friend now is an investment for our future.

✎ A guy who hugely sponsored a girl through school only to "lose" her to another man after her education got deadly disappointed. A lady who spent all her savings to set up this guy, who later dumped her, ended up an emotional wreck. Don't be selfish or foolish. Love is a relationship and not a business investment.

29. I am not interested in dating any girl until I have built a house of my own.

   - It is a good plan to have a property of your own but making it a precondition for getting married may amount to a poor sense of judgment which results to unnecessary delay. God's Word counsels that, if you wait for perfect conditions, you will never get anything done.5

30. I don't think I am ready to discuss marriage now with any man because my elder sister is not yet married.

🖎 God's plan and time table for two separate individuals is not the same. It might be the culture of your community not to give out the younger before the older girl; however the Scripture does not support such tradition.6

31. My pastor says no, maybe he is arranging her for Brother X. I am leaving that church.

🖎 All things work together for good, stay submissive to spiritual authority and God will exalt you in due time. You may at a later time discover the reason for your pastor's position.

Chapter Three

THE GIRL OF MY DREAM

How Do I Find Her?

He, who finds a wife, finds a good thing and obtains favor from the Lord.....

The process of getting a wife requires finding, which implies seeking, looking for, or searching. This is because ladies are everywhere but wives are "hidden". Good qualities are not usually kept on the surface hence the need for a diligent search.

Learn To Trust the Holy Spirit

God Himself is the author of marriage; therefore anyone who wants to go into it should trust Him to activate it. Going into marriage without the guidance of the Holy Spirit is like a tourist in a strange land without a guide. God knows the best for you and he wants you to have that best. King

Solomon says..." a prudent wife is from the Lord. The Message translation puts it this way"...a congenial spouse comes straight from God". Congenial means 'pleasant in a way that makes you feel comfortable and relaxed'. You don't need to be very spiritual to be led by the Holy Spirit, especially in this issue. Just sincerely depend on God to guide your and commit yourself to biblical principles.

Humility And Patience Will Always Win.

You must be humble to be able to locate a wife. You may need to go a longer distance with some ladies to prove your seriousness. Proud and arrogant men often miss out here and find it difficult to get good wives.

The art of wooing a lady you really admire demands patience, level headedness and tolerance. Sometimes relationships that work pass through the crucible of persistence. It is part of feminine demeanor to show initial reluctance before manifesting any sign of acceptance.

Be bold and know what you want. Don't be intimidated at any time. Go for what you want, with a high level of confidence without compromising gentlemanliness. Know exactly what you want, the kind of person you need. Ladies show respect to men who know what they want from the onset and are bold about it.

> **Real love is more than a beautiful feeling - it's a commitment**

12 Qualities You Must Look Out For

The list is actually inconclusive but I will mention only twelve, basic features.

1. Does She Love God Genuinely?

She must sincerely love the Lord and the gospel. It is the quality of her relationship with God that reflects in her relationship with men which includes submission to her husband. The stability of every home and level of peace between couples is strongly related to the understanding and obedience to the word of God guiding relationships.

2. Does She Love Your Personality?

She must love your company not because of what you have or what you can provide. She should be someone who celebrates you and not merely tolerating your presence. She should be your No 1 cheer leader even when you don't have much success yet. Also beware of fleece-chasers (feminine for gold-diggers)

3. Does She Encourage Your Vision?

She must be interested in the things that drive you, your passion, dreams and ideals (I don't mean frivolities). Initially she might not necessarily be excited as you are about them; however a good level of expressed interest must be visible.

4. Does She Have Respect for Family Values?

Though rare to find the contrary, a good wife must exhibit regards for family life. Every mother is first a home-maker. Don't be carried away during casual interactions, look out for homeliness, mother-attitudes, and good household etiquettes

> There are some young ladies who want to be married, but don't really want to be a wife and a mother.

She must not essentially be like your mother or your pastor's wife but her unique good self. Most times these qualities are initially found in their crude form.

5. What's Her Attitude with Money?

In Africa especially, women are known for their industry and thrift. Does she encourage savings or is she a spendthrift? Some relationships that started well begin to face challenges when the income could not match the extravagant desires of the wives. Be sure you do not go into marriage with a lady whose style of living is far higher than yours unless you are prepared to upgrade. This is because you may never be able to satisfy her.

6. Does Her Life Ambition Suit Yours?

You make a grievous mistake when you take for granted that your wife's ambition or career does not matter so long as you are the head of the home! Two cannot walk together except they agree. Let it be discussed and agreed upon before marriage what she wants and her understanding of your own view. If her career and yours clash then your marriage, children and home might suffer. Sometimes it gives room to strained relationship or outright divorce.

7. What's Her Threshold Attraction?

She must be beautiful and attractive in your eyes. Beauty they say is in the eyes of the beholder. What one man describes as beautiful in a particular woman might be quite different from another man's parameter. You must establish your own threshold attraction. What can you say that makes her attractive to you? If you are regenerated and your mind renewed, the Holy Spirit puts a particular good feature for you to look for in a life partner. Be sure your threshold attraction is not a fading statistics.

8. Is She Transparent And Honest?

In today's world, people have no respect for sincerity. Many people are living false lives. Be magnanimous and godly enough to accommodate her ugly past (if any) as she discloses them to you. Probe every shady situation or suspicions activities now and move ahead if applicable.

9. What Can You Say About Her Character?

Charm is deceptive and beauty is fleeting, but a woman who fears the Lord is to be praised.3 When everything has faded- elegance, physical beauty, charisma etc, it is only character and attitude that

> A woman wants a man she can look up to, but one who will not look down on her.

define a good wife. Choose character over body shape, glamour and status.

10. Does She Compliment Your Personality?

God said ".... I will make him a helpmeet comparable to him."4 Are you compatible? What is your personality type? Is it Sanguine, choleric, phlegmatic or melancholy? Watch out, most couples who thought they share some similarities in their likes and dislikes have discovered otherwise after marriage. Differences in your backgrounds, education, upbringing and intelligence may lead to strong disagreement on essential viewpoints. When choosing a life partner do not ignore these factors. Your stands on vital issues such as money, children, manners, family, religious pursuit, social events, dress-codes, best food and so on should be unselfishly harmonized.

11. What Is Her Stand On Traditional Beliefs & Myths Of Her People?

Find out what her people do practice that are opposed to the Word of God and know what her opinion is about them. This is much more important if you are African getting married to an African and she is not from same tribe with you. Some believers have not renewed their minds in line with God's Word concerning traditional beliefs. I once handled a situation where they believe that if your wife is the first daughter, before she gives birth to your first child you must present a male goat to the father about the fifth month of the first pregnancy otherwise she will experience stillbirth. Before this couple met me they had lost a seven-month pregnancy. Thank God, they now have as many as they wanted because we prayed and broke the demonic hold of such myth on them.

12. Antecedents and Spiritual Dimension

Finally, if the girl of your dream comes from backgrounds such as, broken home, polygamous or single parent and/or you share either of the backgrounds above, do not take things for granted. Reach out to your minister and let appropriate spiritual action be taken to disconnect your relationship from the history of your bloodline. Biblical counseling for both of you is also very important even as you renew your mind with the Word of God. The environment and nature of our upbringing affects our mindsets on issues.

If you do not replace the views about family life you got from your parents (especially faulty ones), you might see them repeating in your own home.

Chapter Four

THE SUITOR NEXT DOOR

How Do I Recognize Him?

Scarcely had I passed them when I found the one my heart loves. I held him and would not let him go till I had brought him to my mother's house, to the room of the one who conceived me.

Almost every single that is ready for marriage struggles with questions like, how can I find the right person? How do I recognize and hook Mr. Right...?

Actually in my opinion, locating a life partner these days poses a more critical challenge to women than it does for men. Traditionally, ladies do not approach men for marriage. A lady may admire a guy as much as pray but it takes the initiative of the man to turn the admiration into a reality. All classes of women can encounter these challenges whether rich, poor, beautiful, educated, working class, not well educated, young, old, enlightened, timid, spiritual or worldly.

- Generally, age is more of a threat to a woman than it is to a man when it comes to marriage. A 50year old man can easily marry a 25year old woman but the reverse comes as a miracle. Women think of menopause...

- Women more often fall victims of relationship fraud than men because of presumption. Women seem to be more anxious...

✒ It is proven that more men ditch their girlfriends than women do their male friends. Women think more of commitment...

✒ It is very rare for a woman to deceive a man into marriage with monetary inducements unlike some men who lure vulnerable ladies into marrying them with material gratification and cosmetic lifestyle. It seems women are more economically disadvantaged...

✒ More men have deceived their female friends, even followed them to churches and became members, pretending to be good believes only to show their true colors after the wedding. Most sisters are simply naïve

✒ Women mean affection and care when they talk love while most men think sex within the same context. It seems women understand love more them men...

Without the help of God the above scenarios and more make it more difficult for women to really determine who is genuine, whom to love and commit their hearts to.

Consequently, three important dispositions are necessary as you proceed on this journey.

✎ Let God lead you.

Allow the Holy Spirit to lead and guide you. You need to maintain a personal father-child relationship with God. Spend time to study the word of God and be prayerful out of your love for God not just because you need a life partner. Most people who begin to seek God only when they are in need move from one place to another and become more confused. Delight yourself in the Lord. Be kingdom-minded.

✎ Pay attention to 'You'.

Be a focused person. Know what you want and where you are going in life. It will help you choose the right man. (You can't travel with a man who is not going your direction and not miss your way. If you don't stand for something you fall for anything.2

Develop the qualities that attract men in women like femininity, affirmation, encouragement and tenderness. Keep your distance. Recognize that fundamental anomaly of human nature; we prize what we cannot easily get. We take for granted and even come to despise that which costs us no effort. Put value on 'You'. You are not cheap. You are, not out-dated. You are marvelously crafted and designed by God himself.

✎ The man you want or the Man you need..?

The man you marry is as important as your future. He is as important as your children yet unborn. He is as important as your salvation! Having the picture of the kind of husband you want is very important but not as important as the kind of man you need

> "What we need today are more young men who are not afraid of being real, authentic, and committed to a young lady in a relationship".

12 Qualities You Look Out For

1. How is His Relationship with God?

How often does he go to church? Does he go to church because you want him to or because he is in love with God? Does he read the Word of God? How often does he pray? When and how? Can you prove his love for God? A man who genuinely loves God will love and

respect his wife. DO NOT MARRY AN UNBELIEVER thinking you will change him later!

2. What kind of Company does he keep?

He must exhibit the ability to choose good companies and generally make good decisions. Who are his close pals? "Show me your friends and I will tell you who you are," an old maxim readily comes to mind. The Bible says that he that walks with the wise shall be wise but the companion of fools shall be destroyed. Where does he spend most of his spare time?

3. Is He Honest?

Honesty is an asset exhibited only by the bold. Truthfulness to oneself is the foundation to a life of honesty. Do his words mean anything to him? Does he keep promises and appointments? Is he reliable in little matters? Honest people do not make many promises yet they are promise keepers. They are not perfect but are transparent in their dealings. Is he consistent with information? You don't need a life time to discover a dishonest person. Watch carefully.

4. How is His Emotional Life?

How does he express anger, displeasure or frustration? Is it in a positive or negative way? You can always evaluate one's state of heart or personality by the way he expresses emotions. Is he temperamental? Does he bear grudges? Can you cope with an irrational person as a husband?

5. Is He Friendly?

One of the greatest challenges marriages face today is when two persons who were not friends become husband and wife. Is he a good listener? Is he a conversationalist or an "instructor or a dictator"? Does he value and appreciate your opinion? How does he react when you criticize or disagree with his views? Is he your "boss" or your friend? Friends irrespective of age difference laugh together, plan together, exchange views without inhibitions, feel pain together, and love at all times -both in good and bad times.

6. Is He Resourceful?

Does he have a defined direction in life? Purpose, vision, hard work and focus should define the man. His present financial or social capacity is not as important as where he's headed. Much more important is what he is presently doing to achieve his destination. Does he think up solutions or over-emphasize challenges? Does he take responsibility or shift blame or push up excuses?

Don't marry an idle or a lazy man no matter how handsome and well-dressed. Beware of men with sweet

tongues and weak hands. They talk big and achieve little or nothing.

7. Is He Generous and Caring?
Selfishness kills relationships. A man does not need to be rich to be generous. It is a matter of the heart. He gives love, care, attention and counsel. Does he think about your welfare? Does he show positive interests in your general development? Does he easily take notice of things that bother you without invitation?

8. Is He Family Minded?
How often does he ask of your parents, siblings and friends? Does he side-line discussions about his family? What level of respect does he show towards

his parents and yours? Is he proud to introduce you to his friends and close relatives? Beware when he tells you that all his family members stay abroad. A man who keeps on postponing meeting with your parents, seeing your pastor or taking you to his own pastor should not be regarded as a serious suitor.

9. Is He Gentle?

That a man is always quiet does not translate to being gentle. A gentleman is not a university graduate or a company executive or a well dressed working-class car owner. Is he polite and respectful? Does he treat

people especially ladies with dignity? Does he threaten, scream, shout or insult? A man who beats his girlfriend because he was provoked (though he apologies later) might go very brutal by the time they are married. Does he have the boldness to say "I'm sorry," when he is wrong?

10. What Job Does He Do?

What does he do for a living? How exactly does he make his money? Find out. Just because you met him in the church does not make him a responsible citizen. It is dangerous to date a man whose source of income you cannot verify. Don't be blindfolded by his gifts.

11. Who is His Mentor or Role Model?

Does he have a pastor? Does he submit to any spiritual authority? Who? A man who has no mentor, no specific pastor (but moves around one 'prophet' or another), attends no specific church as an established member; does not pay his tithe or pays anytime and anywhere he likes is a dangerous man. He is responsible to no one. You will not be safe with him as head of your home. That home will definitely be porous spiritually and of course financially.

12. Is He The Kind of Man You Respect?

One of the most essential ingredients you cannot afford to trade for anything is that your potential spouse must merit your respect. Never should you marry a man you cannot respect; that would amount to spending your life in frustration.

"A man who keeps on postponing meeting your pastor, your parents, or introducing you to his close relations may not be a serious suitor..."

Chapter Five

ANSWERS TO 31 CRITICAL QUESTIONS

Good understanding gains favor....Every prudent man acts with knowledge...

1. How do I find the will of God?

Close your eyes and pray. Then open your eyes and watch diligently! It is God's responsibility to lead you while it is yours to follow and then find. You are to look to god to guide you and you are to use the common sense and wisdom He has given you.

First renew your mind on the purposes of marriage in the light of God's Word. God designed marriage for companionship, complimentary, partnership, procreation, sexual pleasure, fulfillment of kingdom purpose, etc.

Then ask God fora life partner. Be sincere
You do not start praying for God's will when you are already 'fallen in passion' with a sister. You can't hear or

see anything but what your heart admires at that time. The best time to seek God's face is early in your rapport, when even if you lose the relationship you won't hurt. By then your heart is unbiased and willing to follow instructions. Apart from spiritual search, be sure the kind of person you are looking for. Get busy with your assignment and work. Relax in God's hands- trust the Holy Spirit to assist you -no worries, no anxiety. When perplexed, seek counsel.

> **"God's will and what is best for you are one and the same thing - George Eager"**

2. I am convinced that she is the will God for me but she has refused to date me. What do I do?

Search for the will of God in marriage still remains inconclusive until she comes to terms with you. Sometimes what most people call the will of God is their strong desire that has lasted for a long time or even a dream of the night arising from mental conception and admiration or somebody's highly respected opinion which they consider sacred. Make sure yours has passed through the crucible of the above scenario and still stands.

Note that the will of God is not as difficult as portrayed through some people's experiences. It is also true that some ladies may not willingly agree at the onset. That's why the spirit alone does not conclude whom you marry. Wooing belongs to the wisdom of the mind (soul). Be friendly and courteous. Look at your self- image, packaging and general attitude especially towards ladies.

Make sure you are not a selfish type. Show interest in her passion and future. Find out her challenges and unconditionally try to assist. Don't pressurize her with gifts, money or phone calls.

Sincerely if you have done all these without appreciable result, leave her alone for some (good) time.

3. Is it true that God has a particular girl for a particular man to marry, if one misses her, he has missed his destiny?

It is not exactly like that. In fact, it you miss her you can remain single and still fulfill a colorful destiny. Marriage is not all there is to life. However this is not a license for guess work when looking for life a partner.

Some folks box themselves into a tight corner by the reason of wrong beliefs founded on people's opinion or traditions of men. On a more serious note, yes it is true

that God (omniscient and loving father) has a specific spouse for a specific person but that does not mean he has made us robots. God gives man the free will to find his spouse. It however depends on factors such as your, relationship with the Holy Spirit, your personality, your location around the time of your desire, your vocation, etc.

God does not impose spouse on anybody but he guides. Sometime even with our mistakes he works out His perfect will and fulfillment for His children.

4. **I am afraid to go into marriage because someone once said, 'if you fail in marriage you have failed in 50% of your life'. Is it true?**

First realize that fear is of the devil. It has torment (evil consequences) and you cannot fear and walk in faith at the same time. Spend time delighting yourself in the Lord; you will notice that purpose will replace fear of failure. Thirdly, tell yourself, "I will not make mistake and I will not fail", "I can marry and succeed". Move closer to people who enjoy good marriage relationship. Seek counsel.

Do not spend time meditating on failed relationships or what people said about 'bad' husbands or wives. Meditate on what God's Word says.

5. The Lord revealed to me that Brother X is going to be my husband but he has refused to talk. What do I do?

Truly if the Lord spoke to you, the guy will in one way or the other approach you. Remember '... He that believeth shall not make haste'. Be patient. And pray that God speaks to him too. See also answer to Q2. Secondly, be careful about "the Lord says..." Be sure it is not your mind (which must not necessarily be evil). Again make sure too that you are not wasting your time on someone who is on course to another destination altogether. Please seek counsel from your pastor or a marriage counselor.7

6. **I sincerely admire this guy, we are very friendly and 'flow' very well. I don't really mind him for the father of my children but he does not seem to be thinking that way. Do I propose to him, how?**

In some cultures of the world, you may go ahead and proposed to him. However around our African cultures, it is rare. I advise you withdraw a little bit from him, make yourself scarce in case he is taking his time and still studying you. Do not assume or day-dream in order to avoid unnecessary emotional breakdown in case he has no marriage plans at all.

Most powerfully, pray about it in order to keep your mind sound and mortify the flesh in case you're lost in lust. Keep off! After all these if the "sincere admiration" continues mention it to your Pastor's wife or an elderly godly woman, NOT your girlfriend or another single male friend!

7. **My parent/s said if I marry him/her, they will disown me and I love him/her. Do you think I should defy my parents and go ahead or dump him/her?**

If you really love him/her, patiently wait and get their consent (it carries a special blessing). Seek and apply all wisdom, meet and use people that they respect and value and above all pray, pray and pray that God should touch their hearts. If you just quit because your parents said no, the love may not actually be there.

Another very important reason you should pray (fervently and sincerely) is that opposition sometimes could be an opportunity for God to show us what we hitherto failed to see. If your fiancé becomes impatient, disrespectful (by attitude) and vituperative about your parents' stand, watch out!

8. **She had a child some years ago while in school, now she is born again. I love her can I propose to her?**

Yes you can, provided you have settled some issues. Who is the father of her child, does he claim paternity? Is she still in touch with the ex-? Are you sincerely ready to father that child as your first child if the above issues are resolved?

All things being equal having ascertained the mind of God, decide the number of children you want to have reckoning with the one she is coming with. Settle these matters carefully. Do not handle them hastily, lightly or in isolation. Pray, investigate, and be persuaded.

9. He beats me most times we have a quarrel. He always comes begging and because I don't want to lose him I forgive him. Do you think he will make me happy?

A good husband material must have respect for the sanctity of womanhood. Most men who best their girlfriends end up as wife batterers. If the guy you are dating is driven by uncontrolled anger resulting in violence he should not be considered matured for marriage no matter his age.

10. How do I get him to propose? He visits and eats regularly in my house; friendly, but wouldn't want to discuss marriage.

My dear, it is quite unfortunate that some guys take undue advantage of anxious and vulnerable ladies. I will advise you never to assume that every close relationship with the opposite single leads to marriage. However to get him to define his mission follow these steps: Find a way to discourage his frequent visits. Shut your kitchen "half-way". You can go visiting a

girlfriend, a family or some other place at the time he comes (I hope he doesn't call late night!)

Do not discuss marriage or show desperation any time he is around, even in the midst of other friends.

Make yourself scarce and verify that he is not a user; users are dumpers. Shine your eyes.

11. Which is the best way to propose to a lady you want to marry?

There are several right ways of making a girl know you want to marry her. My advice is that you make it as simple as possible. Make it clear, direct, natural and romantic.

One school of thought believes that you must soberly invite her may be to a church auditorium, pray first and say something like, "The Lord has revealed to me that you will be my wife" or "I have been waiting on the Lord since....the Holy Spirit told me that you are my life partner". Some even say after a very powerful prayer session with her (do not ask me what the prayer point is), you give her a Bible; from there she will understand what you mean.

Like I said earlier, keep it simple. Don't try to show her how spiritual you are or the detail of how you received it from God, unless she asks for your validation. As soon as you are sure of the will of God, invite her (fix a suitable meeting place) may be over a lunch or just in any friendly environment.

Looking straight into her eyes, say something like "please will you marry me", "I love you and will like to spend the rest of my life with you". Some do it with a ring but not without finishing some psychological underground work! Anyhow keep it simple, brief, interesting, romantic, natural and at the same time give her the opportunity to respond at her own pace and time.

12. **God says he will give us the desires of our heart. How come all the guys that approach me for marriage are either non-believers or far below my expectations?**

What are your expectations? I hope it does not fall outside God's standard? What type of company do you enjoy and how are you dressed? Unfortunately men look at outward appearance before they think inside. The issue of marriage is not different. Dead bodies and dirty environments attract flies.

Reexamine your conducts, reappraise your costumes and reposition your company. Define your expectations from God's perspective, be willing to do

His will and go ahead, and ask him for a good life partner.

13. He jilted me four years ago, broke my heart because of another girl, now he is back begging I should marry him. What do I do?

Let a third party, preferably your pastor/counselor hear his reasons for jilting you from his own mouth. Carefully evaluate the validity of his repentance and articulate reason for coming back to you. Examine his motive critically, without sentiments. Please do not be in a hurry about this no matter how desperately you need a husband. It is possible his remorse is genuine and also possible he has not learnt his lessons. You are too precious to be toyed with. Lastly how has he detached from the other girl? May God help you.

14. I am born again, my guy is a staunch catholic, caring and generous. My friends say he is not the best for me. What do I do?

Your friends said that he is not the best for you, what do you say yourself? Not just your friends... not just his care and generosity, your faith must be agreeable, both of you must share the same major perspective about God and life after death in order to make a good and happy couple. A couple must share same definition of pursuit for salvation and godliness in order to be fruitful spiritually and bring up godly children.

15. Must I tell my pastor before I propose to a lady?

As a committed born again child of God, depending on the guideline for getting married in your church, your

pastor or head of marriage department or any other person so designed by the leadership of the church should be informed as soon as it is conceived. This counsel may sound old fashioned but my practical counsel to any serious single desiring to get a life partner irrespective of your spiritual height, social standing or accomplishments is let your pastor or at least a qualified counselor assist you. It is however noteworthy that you should not abdicate your responsibility of choosing your life partner to your pastor (or prophet, as the case may be) he is there as an umpire or guide. Mature counselors /pastors serve as a good bridge between the aspiring spouses. The pastor/counselor must be spirit-filled, God fearing and above all, seen to be unbiased.

16. Is there anything as love at first sight?

Yes and no! One elderly man puts it this way, "Love at first sight is cured by a second look. Keep looking". It is possible that you set your eyes on someone for the very first time and get attracted or interested. But love develops not from first sight but from second observation.

Another scenario is that you might meet someone severally without any feeling or attraction. Along the line either out of an encounter with the person's character or common interest over a period of time love

begins to develop. But you cannot truly love a person whom you do not really know.

> You may be attracted to someone at first sight.
> But you cannot genuinely love a person whom you do not really know

17. I am a university graduate and passionately desire a graduate also for a life partner. However, I just fell in love with this beautiful and intelligent girl who is not a graduate. I am confused...?

Follow your heart, not your love! Why do you want a graduate for a wife? Can you do without those reasons for life or do you have the determination, time, patience and fund to get her through university education? If you answer these questions without sentiments, then you are in the best position to make a good decision. Do remember that most times real love must pass through the test of time and flaws.13

18. **I do not feel anything for him/her. Actually I don't think I love him/her but my prophet says he/she is the will of God for me. What do I do?**

In as much as you have this reverence for 'your' prophet remember that it is not your prophet (or your parents in some instances) you are getting married to. The final decision is yours.

It is possible that you may not feel anything for him/her initially, however if the condition of your heart remains the same for a long period I do not think you can live with him/her. Beware of match-making by prophet/parents/prayer partners or even close friends and people whose opinion you respect.14

19. **She quarrels and insults me in the public on every slight provocation but always apologies. Do I still marry her?**

She may have issue with her temperament and disrespect. The essence of courtship actually is to 'expose' each other's weakness and strength in order to achieve compatibility. If she shows a passionate commitment to adjusting her attitude you can assist her achieve success. Seriously speaking if your love is strong to bear her occasional flying-kettle temperament and some disrespect during the marriage then go ahead but if not consider calling off the relationship.15

20. **We are in courtship for about eight months now. Each time we fix a prayer appointment together she/he doesn't show up on one excuse or the other. It has happened several times. Do I ignore this and marry him/her?**

It is a clear signal that he/she is either not interested in prayers or in the relationship or both. For you as a believer, this is dangerous, so I advise you sit with your partner and discuss the issue. Get his/her real reasons for not showing up. Lacking a genuine reason may mean your future is not together.

If you have the slightest doubt about a relationship it is better to go slow or even back away from it

21. His genotype is AS and mine is AS. Can we go ahead with marriage plans?

Before you go ahead please consult a medical doctor together with your partner. It is good to know exactly what you are going in for. However under normal circumstances one out of every four children you have will be a sickler (SS), two carriers (AS) and one free (AA). The choice is yours.

22. Nobody wants to marry me. Does it mean that God doesn't want me to marry?

Your #1 road block is your mindset which reads: "nobody is interested in me". Secondly, your attitude to life and the opposite sex in particular. Change your thinking, adjust your attitude. Learn to love people. Show some interest in other people's challenges and try to help without ulterior motives. Shift attention from your circumstance. Love God and let people know it. Be diligent in your career. Soon your partner will show up.

23. My fiancée died mysteriously two months to our wedding. After six months I got involved with another girl but her parents wanted me to pick a job of their choice contrary to my dream, we separated. I am afraid to propose to any girl now. What do you advise I should do?

No matter what has happened to you, raise your head again knowing that your best stories are yet to be written. Meanwhile remember that fear is Satan's first policemen against his perceived targets. Don't give up on marriage. Prayerfully overcome your fears and get on with your life.

24. I am above 36. No money, no good paying job and I want to get married. How do I go about it?

Do you really plan to get married soon? Have you got a lady that you want to get married to? And what do you consider a good paying job? If you wait for favorable condition you will never get anything started. If you keep telling yourself, "No money", there will be no money! In actual fact, nobody has money; it is vision that attracts money.

Look for a need to meet and you are on your way to making money. Catch a vision, raise your worth. Start working at something beneficial to someone. Think and look positive at life.

25. I hate men. I do not want to hear anything about marriage but my parents (especially my mum) and friends are disturbing me. Must every woman marry?

My dear, your situation looks more serious than expressed. First you need to seek God's healing grace to deal with past hurts, traumas or imbibed negative mindsets. Sometimes it may be as a result of abuse as a child/adolescent, rape or you grew up with a dad who ill-treated your mum. It may also be a case of series of frustrated love relationships. You need the love of Jesus to heal your heart and rid it of hurts and bitterness. I advise you confide in a counselor other than your parents.

God has designed every woman to feel love, fall in love and to enjoy sex -only provided within the confines of marriage and to reproduce. Marriage is honorable.18 God created woman to complement man.

26. I had a girlfriend some years ago as an unbeliever we later separated. Now that I am born again (and in love with a sister whom am getting married to soon) she appears, born-again too and says she still loves me. What do I do?

Tell her you are now in a serious relationship and set for marriage. Discuss it with your fiancée and if possible with your pastor. This increases you commitment to your fiancée. You might feel "something" for her, so avoid any opportunity of seeing, staying or discussing with her. Don't take anything for granted. No secrets now! Be open and honest to her, your fiancée and yourself. This has the potential of either strengthening or destroying your faith and relationship. Please be careful!

"If your love is real, the one you love will bring out your best qualities and make you want to be a better person"

27. Is love actually blind?

Well, if love is blind as they usually say, it is only marriage that opens the eyes!

Agape -unselfish, committed and unconditional is not blind. It sees the faults of the other person but overlooks them.

Eros -erotic, romantic love, love of ideals, pleasures, loving one's friend.

Philos to be fond of, take pleasure in, having personal attachment for someone.

Eros and philos most times can be blind, blind to realities due to overwhelming emotional forces or selfish interests.

Agape does not only issue from God, it was 'shed abroad the heart of believers by the Holy Spirit. It makes the lover seek the highest good of the other person irrespective of his/her responses. It gives freely. It is not blind, it is not stupid but covers multitude of faults.20

28. What does dress code have to do with getting a life partner?

Almost everything! Human beings tend to look at outward appearance all the time. Someone said "you are addressed the way you are dressed". It is true that different people look out for different things in would- be lovers but there are common grounds.

Modesty, decency and knowing what fits should guide your dress-sense. Your dressing must not necessarily be expensive or flamboyant to make good sense. You can't wear a hairdo of 48 year old and expect a youngster to approach you. Tomboys (girls who act and dress like boys all the time) should adjust attitudes if they want to get married. Guys should know how to combine colors and girls please put on what suits your statistics not just fashion.

29. He is not from my tribe and we are in love. How do I cope if we get married?

How have you been coping since you met each other? Well, begin to study and develop interest in each other's dialect, type of food, dressing, family and culture generally. Have a common faith. Discuss and interact freely.

Intertribal marriages can be exciting and is proven to be more stable than that of some culture. There

> "A satisfying marriage with someone you love deeply is one of the richest gifts God can ever give you"

seems to be higher level of respect for each other's views and ideals. If God is behind it, you can cope.

30. **My fiancée earns very much more than I do. Do you think she will be submissive if we get married?**

It depends on a lot of factors. How is your relationship with her now? What is the quality of your communication? How does she talk and relate to you during discussions, especially in the presence of friends?

Secondly you must be willing to work on your personality and self image. Don't get hooked with inferiority complex.

Develop your source of income and make sure it is growing. You should not depend on her income no

matter how much she earns. Be ready to pick up your bills, including taking care of her basic needs. Start it now! Have a mind of your own on issues so that you can be dependable. Marriage is not only about money and income. Without blackmail or threatening, get her to respect you and do little without your major input. Respect and submission are commanded by God but it is earned by man. Walk in wisdom.21

31. My fiancé is insisting we have sex since we are going to be married soon. He opined that it is not wrong provided we remain faithful to each other. Is he right?

Wrong, very wrong. Most vulnerable and ignorant girls have been blackmailed and lured into sex by their male friends with the guise that, "we will get married soon", only to disappear after series of the act. Even when they do not disappear, it is still fornication and a sin against your flesh and God (your body is the temple of the Holy Spirit).

> "Intimacy between man and woman is God's wedding gift to the newlyweds, and this gift is not to be opened early"

Some have even accused the girls of unfaithfulness because they refuse having sex with them. Some

threatened to break the relationship if the girls do not give in. My dear sister, do not buy into such blackmail or succumb to the threats. Besides, it is more honorable for any girl to say no to sex before marriage. Any man who really loves you will respect your wish and encourage you to stay pure. Moreover there is no guarantee that a guy who insists on having sex before wedlock will not share you with another woman when married.

> "A Christian is one who can wait... Wait for the complete union. By not waiting you will gain nothing and you will lose much. I will put what you would lose into three words: freedom, joy, and beauty.
>
> Walter Trobisch"

Final Word

This plan of mine are not what you would work out, neither are my thoughts the same as yours. Isa 55:8 (TLB)

Trust in the Lord with all your hearts, and lean not on your own understanding, in all your ways acknowledge Him, and He shall direct your paths. Prov. 3:5-6

Delight yourself also in the LORD, and He shall give you the desires of your heart. Psa. 37:4

The choice you make today is the chance you have tomorrow to challenge your circumstances. Do not make your choices in a hurry or in ignorance. You will have no excuse whatsoever if you fail. Why? You have information act on them. You have time now do not waste it. You have the Holy Spirit let Him guide you. Practically READ this book at least 12 good times within 1 year and YOU will get THE BEST that GOD HAS FOR YOU.

Now the sincere confession of your heart will be: "The Lord will work out His plans for my life for Your loving-kindness, Lord, continues forever. Do not abandon me for you made me". Psa.138:8 (TLB) THIS IS YOUR YEAR IN JESUS NAME!!!

> "The choice you make today is the chance you have tomorrow to challenge your circumstances."

Note

Chapter One/Mindset for Marriage

1. Matt 12:35(NIV) 2. Rom 12:2

3. Jer 1:11-12

4. Matt 19:6&9

5. Gen 2:24

6. Heb 13:4

7. 1Cor 7:2(MSG)

8. Gen 1:27-28

9. Gen 2:18

Chapter Two/31 Common Assumptions

1. Song 2:15(NLT)

2. Gen 2:25

3. Prov 31:30(MSG) 4. Prov 15:17

5. Eccl 11:4(TLB)

6. Gen 29:25-26

Chapter Three/The Girl of My Dream

1. Prov 18:22

2. Prov 19:14

3. Prov 31:30(NIV)

4. Gen 2:18

5. Heb 7:9-10

Chapter Four/The Suitor Next Door

1. Song 3:4(NIV)

2. 2Cor 6:14

3. 2Cor 6:15

4. Prov 13:20

Chapter Five/31 Critical Questions

1. Prov 13:15-16

2. Gen 2: 21-24

3. Jer 29:13

4. Gen 24:64-65

5. Psa 37:4

6. Phil 4:13&8

7. Isa 28:16

8. Prov 21:1 9. Prov 22:24-25

10. Song 4:7

11. Psa 37:5

12. Prov 15:22 13. Luk 14:28

14. Rom 14:5

15. Prov 21:19 16. 1Cor 10:13

17. Eccl 11:4 18. Heb 13:14

19. Gen 2:24

20. 1Pet 4:8

21. Prov 4:7

22. 1Cor 6:19

23. 1Cor 6:18

How May We Help You?

If you need!
Relationship Advice!
Prayers!

Booking for Speaking
Engagements / Seminars!

Please call our 24-Hours Help
Lines: Tel: +234 8055 143 687

(SMS only)
+234 7033 532 990

Or send your request to:
E-mail: revjoe316@yahoo.com.

Get connected!

IF YOU ARE NOT SAVED YOU ARE NOT SAFE!!!

If you do not know Jesus as your Savior and Lord, simply pray the following prayer in faith and Jesus will be your Lord.

Heavenly Father, I come to You in the name of Jesus. Your Word says, "Whosoever shall call on the name of the Lord shall be saved" and "If you confess with your mouth the Lord Jesus and shall believe in your heart that God has raised him from the dead, you shall be saved"

Acts 2:21; Rom. 10:9)

I take You at Your Word. I confess that Jesus is Lord.

And I believe in my heart that raised Him from the dead.

Thank You for coming into my heart today and for being Lord over my life. Amen

If you prayed the above prayers,
please call: +234 7033 532 990

About SIMER-Nigeria

Society for Intertribal Marriage and Ethnic Re-Integration Established in 2009 to pursue the under-listed Objectives through advocacy, workshops, seminars and enlightenment campaigns.

1. Encouraging intertribal / cross-cultural marriages.

2. Fostering national unity & peaceful coexistence.

3. Building mutual understanding & lasting friendship among ethnic nationalities in Nigeria and beyond.

4. Breaking language barriers through genuine family ties.

5. Protecting the interest of widows/widowers and children from in-law marginalization and oppressive cultural practices.

6. Educating prospective individuals / couples on cross- cultural values, beliefs and mindsets.

7. Enlightening parents on the benefits of intertribal marriage.

8. Establishing and operating info-data banks and counseling centers.

For Enquiries, Participation and/or Support Please Contact:

Tel: +234 8055 143 687(sms only) E-mail: simer2009@ymail.com.

About the AUTHOR

Joe Igboanugo pastor, author, relationship advisor, inspirational speaker and consultant is an insightful teacher of God's Word helping people discover and maximally harness their God-given abilities. His peculiar anointing for helping people connect to their life partners and restoring challenged marriages has left testimonies in the lives of many. Joe who had his first degree in Pure & Industrial Chemistry from the prestigious University of Port Harcourt (1989) and a 1995 PGD in Theology from the famous Redeemed Christian Bible College, founded Changers International Church Inc. Port Harcourt, Nigeria. He is the convener of Ministers Welfare & Prayer Fellowship Int'l and President, Society for Intertribal Marriage and Ethnic Reintegration [SIMER Nigeria]. Author of bestsellers, Unlocking Possibility Mentality, Your Dream Can Change Your World and soon-to-be released Marriage Revolution Code 12, Love SEX & Married Life and Censored For MEN Only! Rev Joe, host of Marriage Revolution Seminars is gladly married to Meg (his associate) and they are blessed with three "nations" Mira Obinna, Cheri Ezenwa and Ada Blossom. They live in Port Harcourt.

Worth Reading!!!

Other Powerful Books By Joe Igboanugo.

Unlocking Possibility Mentality

Blow the lid off your
mindset and let the
Holy Spirit create
an unstoppable atmosphere
for uncommon results in
your life.

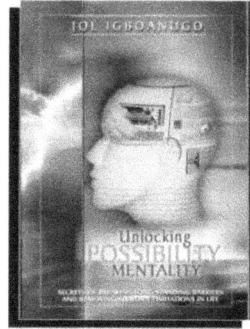

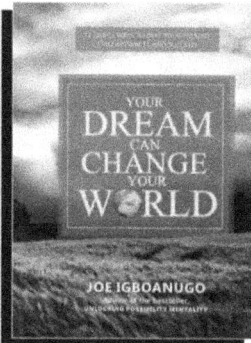

**Your Dream Can Change
Your World**

You can drive your faith
by dreams. This book
shall cause a revolution
in you and launch you
into the best life God has
designed for you.

Making Order

To order this book within Nigeria, visit all leading bookshops, or call / SMS +234 805 514 3687.

To order from outside Nigeria, visit the following websites below, or search online using the book Title or Author name.

Our Official Book Stores

Amazon Book Store, and Kindle store; Author Name/Book Title

CreateSpace Book Store; Author Name/Title.)

Personal Notes